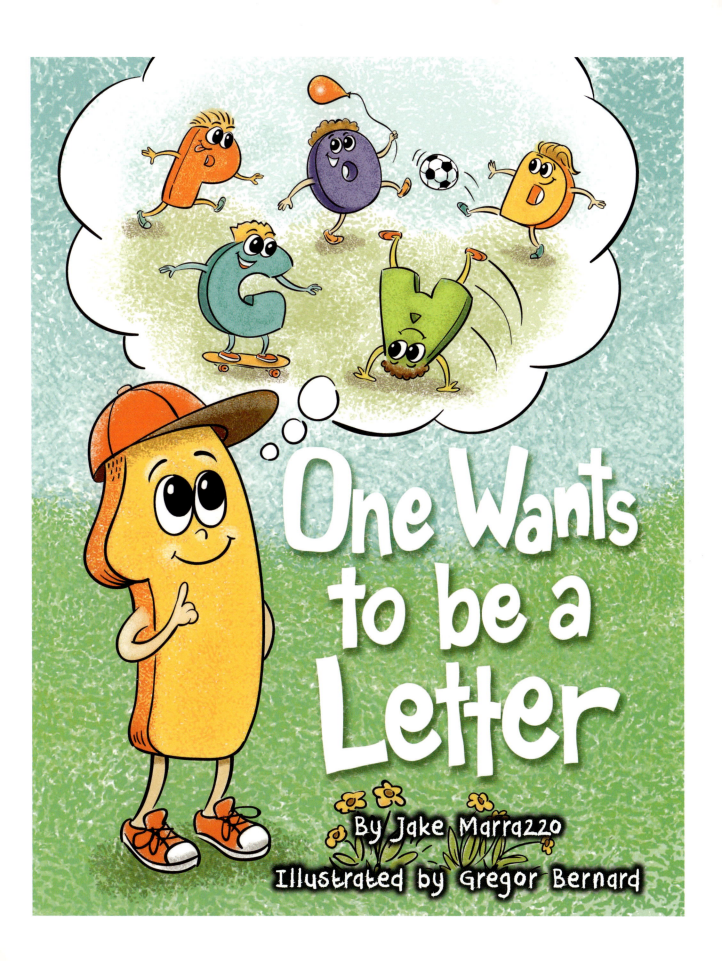

Copyright © 4Jakessake

4jakessake.com

All Rights Reserved. No part of this publication may be reproduced, stored in a retrieval system or transmitted in any form by any means electronic, mechanical, or photocopying, recording or otherwise without permission in writing from the author.

Request for permission to make copies of any part of the work should be submitted online to todd@civinmediarelations.com or Sheryl@4jakessake.com

ISBN: 9780578803845

Imprint: Independently published

Published by Civin Media Relations

www.civinmediarelations.com

To Tyler,

I can't wait to continue to watch you grow.

-Uncle Jake

1 is a number.

But, sometimes he feels like a lonely number.

1 has a lot of friends,
and mostly 1's friends are letters.

This makes 1 a little sad because
1 wants to be like his friends,
1 wants to be a letter.

Letters can do really fun things, like get together and spell words.

Numbers can't do that, they can only get together and make bigger numbers and 1 does not think that is so great.

So one day, 1 decided he was going to be the letter "t". He put his arms out to his sides and walked around all day telling everyone, "Hey, I'm not a number; I am the letter t".

But after a while, 1's arms got tired, and he was just a number again.

The next day, 1 decided to walk around with a ball on his head. "Hey everyone", 1 yelled, "I'm not a number anymore, I am the letter i".

But 1 could not keep the ball balanced on his head. The ball kept falling off, and 1 kept becoming a number again.

1's letter friends kept laughing at him. They said, "1, you cannot be a letter, you are just a number."

This made 1 very sad.

One day, the town was having the annual carnival. Part of the carnival was a race where the fastest contestant won a big trophy.

1 decided to sign up for the race.

On the day of the race, 1 and all his letter friends lined up at the starting line.

"On your mark" yelled the starter. "Get Set" All the racers prepared to run. "GO!" Everyone started to run.

It was crowded, and all the racers kept bumping into each other.

The letters were not built as sleekly as 1. When they tried to run fast, most of them fell over.

But 1 was built straight and narrow. He ran faster and faster and pulled out in front of everyone.

1 easily won the race!

At the award ceremony, 1 was given the biggest trophy he had ever seen. It was gold and blue. At the bottom it said "First Place", and when he looked at the top, it had a giant "#1".

All of 1's friends were happy for him, but they were also a little jealous. They all wanted to be #1.

1 really liked his letter friends,
but now 1 loved being a number.

THE END

About 4 Jake's Sake

A portion of the proceeds from this book will go to the 4 Jake's Sake Charitable Foundation. 4 Jake's Sake started as a team name for a walkathon in 2012. 4 Jake's Sake has since become a non-profit 501 (c)(3) charitable foundation whose main purpose is to help families living with Duchenne Muscular Dystrophy make their homes and lives more accessible. Please visit our website www.4jakessake.com and follow us on social media to see what we are up to.

About the Author— *Jake Marrazzo*

Photograph by Chad Crogan
www.chadcroganphotography.com

From the time Jake learned to speak, it was apparent he was extremely creative. He would constantly be coming up with ideas for books (we read a lot with him especially in his early years). Many times, his ideas would be loosely based on another book or movie he had seen. One morning when Jake was four, he came downstairs and said "Dad, I have an idea for a book and it's called ***One Wants to Be a Letter***. It instantly caught my attention as I knew we did not read a book or watch a movie that had a common theme. So I asked him "What is the story about?" He began to tell me about the number one whose friends were all letters and he felt different and wanted to be like them. What kid or young adult does not feel like this at some point in his life? We talked about the ideas that eventually became this book. Many of the words came from me, but the idea and story came from the creative mind of a four year old.

There is a bit of prophecy here, as Jake was diagnosed with Duchenne Muscular Dystrophy when he was eight, and lost his ability to walk when he was twelve. At the time of publishing, Jake is 17 and going into his senior year of high school (yes, it did take thirteen years after the story idea to get to publishing). And despite his physical challenges, he still wants to be just like everyone else.

- John Marrazzo, aka Jake's Dad

About the Publisher— Todd Civin

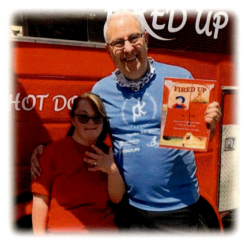

Todd Civin is a husband, father of five and grandfather of four to date. He is a graduate of Syracuse University Newhouse School of Public Communications. Todd is the owner and creator of Civin Media Relations and is the Social Media Director for the Kyle Pease Foundation and the Hoyt Foundation.

He is the co-author of forty books including **One Letter at a Time** by Rick Hoyt, **Destined to Run** by Wes Harding, **Just My Game** by MLB pitcher Jason Grilli, **Line Change** by Matt Brown, **Beyond the Finish** by Brent and Kyle Pease and 121 Days by Sadie Raymond. He is also the creator of dozens of children's books among them **Where There's a Wheel There's a Way, A Knight in Shining Armor, A Bike to Call Their Own, Together We Finish!, MacKenzie; Baby She Was Born to Mother and A Cup of Kindness.** He is thrilled to add **One Wants to be a Letter** to the every growing CMR library of books.

About the Artist—Gregor Bernard

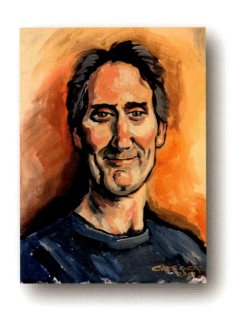

Gregor is a Commercial Artist who grew up in Massachusetts and now lives in Milford, NH. Since 1995 he has provided artwork in tradition mediums such as watercolor, pen and ink and the digital platform. Drawing inspiration from artists like Arthur Rackham and Mort Drucker, creating whimsical fun characters that illustrate ideas and stories is a passion of his. Gregor has created award winning editorial cartoons and magazine covers, best selling advertising illustration and story books for many delighted customers. When not in his studio Gregor can be found hiking, biking and skiing the trails of New England.

Hey, Gregor We think you're ...

Acknowledgements

There are many people who I'd like to acknowledge.

Thank you Gregor for drawing these great illustrations you saw in this book. I feel that your illustrations captured the vision I had for this story way back in 2007.

Thank you to Todd, for allowing my children's book to become a reality.

Thank you to my parents, who also helped me make this idea a reality, and being major influences in my life.

Thank you to my brother Cletus and my sister Katelynn, you didn't live in the same house as me for very long, but you both were always a big influence on me.

Thank you to my brother in-law Ryan for being an amazing husband to my sister and never failing to make me laugh.

Thank you to my niece Ellie and my nephew Tyler, you two brighten up my day whenever I see you and I can't wait to see you continue to grow.

Thank you to my Nana, some of my fondest memories have been going out to restaurants with you, thank you for being a great grandparent.

Thank you to Papa and Pat, I have always enjoyed watching the birds with you.

Thank you to my caretaker and friend Tim, thank you for an amazing five years of laughter and joy.

Thank you to my para Jen Libby, you have made high school so enjoyable for me over the past four years of my life, and have never failed to make me laugh.

Thank you to my instructors that help run my schools drama program, Mrs. McKenzie, Scott, Rachel, and Deb, you have been major influences on my life over the past few years, thank you for the music.

Thank you to all of my friends, I love you all so much.

Thank you to my next-door neighbors Chad, Keri, Josh, Alex, Brady, and Caden, some of the fondest memories I've ever had have been with all of you, thank you for everything.

A special shout out to **Elbow Grease Marketing** and Olivier Sartor for his tireless effort and patience in helping us with this project. www.elbowgreasemarketing.com

Thank you to my instructors over at the summer performing arts program I have performed for, Alyssa, Jay, and Steven, all three of you have been amazing instructors and are incredible human beings.

And finally, thank you all for reading…

You asked for it and we have opened it! One Wants to be a Letter book has launched an online store of merchandise. All you fans of One and his Letter Friends can grab some official merchandise by heading to the link below.

www.4-jakes-sake.myshopify.com